D1223090

What's So Great About . . . ?

ROSA PARKS

Jim Whiting

Mitchell Lane
PUBLISHERS

P.O. Box 196
Hockessin, Delaware 19707
Visit us on the web: www.mitchelllane.com
Comments? email us: mitchelllane@mitchelllane.com

Mitchell Lane PUBLISHERS

Printing   1   2   3   4   5   6   7   8   9

A Robbie Reader/What's So Great About . . . ?

Amelia Earhart	Anne Frank	Annie Oakley
Christopher Columbus	Daniel Boone	Davy Crockett
Elizabeth Blackwell	Ferdinand Magellan	Francis Scott Key
Galileo	George Washington Carver	Harriet Tubman
Helen Keller	Henry Hudson	Jacques Cartier
Johnny Appleseed	Paul Bunyan	Robert Fulton
Rosa Parks	Sam Houston	

Library of Congress Cataloging-in-Publication Data
Whiting, Jim.
   Rosa Parks / by Jim Whiting.
      p. cm. — (A Robbie reader, what's so great about . . . ?)
   Includes bibliographical references and index.
   ISBN 978-1-58415-573-7 (library bound)
   1. Parks, Rosa, 1913–2005—Juvenile literature. 2. African American women—Alabama—Montgomery—Biography—Juvenile literature. 3. African Americans—Alabama—Montgomery—Biography—Juvenile literature. 4. African Americans—Civil rights—Alabama—Montgomery—History—20th century—Juvenile literature.
5. Segregation in transportation—Alabama—Montgomery—History—20th century—Juvenile literature. 6. Montgomery (Ala.)—Race relations—Juvenile literature.
7. Montgomery (Ala.)—Biography—Juvenile literature. I. Title.
F334.M753P3887 2008
323.092—dc22
[B]   2007000785

ABOUT THE AUTHOR: Jim Whiting has been a remarkably versatile and accomplished journalist, writer, editor, and photographer for more than 30 years. He has written and edited more than 250 nonfiction children's books. His subjects range from authors to zoologists and include contemporary pop icons and classical musicians, saints and scientists, emperors and explorers. Representative titles include *The Life and Times of Franz Liszt, The Life and Times of Julius Caesar, Charles Schulz, Charles Darwin and the Origin of the Species, Juan Ponce de Leon, Robert Fulton, Anne Frank,* and *The Scopes Monkey Trial.* He lives in Washington State with his wife and two teenage sons.

PHOTO CREDITS: Cover, p. 18—National Archives and Records Administration; pp. 1, 3, 22—Associated Press/Library of Congress; p. 4—AP Photo/Montgomery County Sheriff's Office; p. 6—Henry Ford Museum; pp. 7, 21—Library of Congress; pp. 8, 9—Records of the District Court of the United States National Archives and Records Administration; pp. 10, 20—Don Cravens/Time Life Pictures/Getty Images; p. 14—AP Photo/Gene Herrick; p. 17—Grey Villet/Time Life Pictures/ Getty Images; p. 25—Richard Ellis/AFP/Getty Images; p. 26—Paul Sancya/AFP/Getty Images; p. 27—Mandel Ngan/AFP/Getty Images.

PPC

TABLE OF CONTENTS

Words in **bold** type can be found in the glossary.

POLICE DEPARTMENT
CITY OF MONTGOMERY

Date 12-1-55 19___

Complainant J.F.Blake (wm)

Address 27 No.Lewis St.   Phone No.___

Offense Misc.   Reported By Same as above

Address ___   Phone No.___

Date and Time Offense Committed 12-1-55   6:06 pm

Place of Occurrence In Front of Empire Theatre (On Montgomery Street)

Person or Property Attacked ___

How Attacked ___

Person Wanted ___

Value of Property Stolen ___   Value Recovered ___

Details of Complaint (list, describe and give value of property stolen)

We received a call upon arrival the bus operator said he had a colored female

sitting in the white section of the bus, and would not move back.

We (Day & Mixon) also saw her.

The bus operator signed a warrant for her. Rosa Parks, (cf) 634 Cleveland Court.

Rosa Parks (cf) was charged with chapter 6 section 11 of the Montgomery City Code.

Warrant #14254

THIS OFFENSE IS DECLARED: Officers J. D. Day
UNFOUNDED   □
CLEARED BY ARREST   □   D. W. Mixon
EXCEPTIONALLY CLEARED □
INACTIVE (NOT CLEARED) □

Division Patrol   Time 7:00 pm
                                              12-1-55

The police report on Rosa Parks. It says, "We received a call upon arrival the bus operator said he had a colored female sitting in the white section of the bus, and would not move back." December 1, 1955, was not the first time Rosa had refused to give up her seat to a white person. The bus driver, J. F. Blake, had thrown her off the bus in 1943 for breaking the same law.

A Famous Bus Ride

On the afternoon of December 1, 1955, Rosa Parks was riding the bus home from work. She was a **seamstress** for a department store in Montgomery, Alabama.

Rosa was African American. At that time, African Americans in the South were usually separated from white people. This practice was called **segregation** (seh-gruh-GAY-shun). They were also treated differently.

Buses were one of the public places where segregation was practiced. African Americans had to sit at the back of the bus. If all the seats were filled and a white person boarded the bus, one of the African Americans would have to stand so that the white person could sit down. That was the law.

On this day, Rosa's bus was full. A white man boarded the bus. The bus driver ordered Rosa to give up her seat. She refused.

The driver stopped the bus and walked back to Rosa. He was angry with her. She wasn't obeying the law.

"Are you going to stand up?" the bus driver asked.

"No," Rosa answered.

The bus that Rosa Parks rode in 1955 was later purchased by the Henry Ford Museum in Detroit, Michigan. It is the center of an exhibition called With Liberty and Justice for All. Museum visitors can sit in the bus and listen to a recording of Rosa Parks explaining why she refused to give up her seat.

"Well, by God, I'm going to have you arrested," the driver shouted.

"You may do that," Rosa said.

Policemen came to the bus. They took Rosa to the police station. She was locked in a jail cell for a few hours.

Thousands of people supported Rosa's decision. Just over a year later, the bus laws in Montgomery were changed. African Americans would no longer have to give up their seats to whites.

Montgomery's bus system was just the start. African Americans wanted to change other unfair laws. They wanted the country to be **integrated** (IN-tuh-gray-ted). That means everyone would receive the same treatment, no matter what their skin color.

Rosa Parks had worked as a seamstress for much of her life before her arrest in 1955. She was fired almost immediately afterward.

Learning to Respect Herself

Rosa McCauley was born on February 4, 1913, in Tuskegee, Alabama. Her father, James McCauley, was a carpenter. Her mother, Leona McCauley, had been a schoolteacher. By the time Rosa was born, Leona had stopped teaching to raise a family. Rosa would have one brother, Sylvester, who was born in 1914.

James left the family while Rosa was still little. Leona took Rosa and Sylvester to live with their grandmother, Rose. Rose had been a slave when she was a girl. Both Leona and Rose taught Rosa to respect herself.

She needed this self-respect. At that time, African Americans were not often given respect. White youngsters often made fun of

Rosa. Schools for African Americans weren't as good as those for white children. Because most African Americans weren't well educated, it was hard for them to find good jobs.

Rosa had to drop out of school to take care of her mother and grandmother. Both were very ill. She began sewing to earn enough money.

In 1931 she met a young barber named Raymond Parks. She especially liked the way he stood up for what he thought was right. They were married in 1932. He encouraged her to finish high school, and she received her **diploma** (dih-PLOH-muh) in 1934.

Rosa wanted to help other African Americans. She joined the National Association for the Advancement of Colored People (NAACP) in 1943. At that time, the NAACP was the most important group fighting for civil rights. They spoke to people at the U.S. War Department about stopping **discrimination** (dis-krih-mih-NAY-shun) against black soldiers in the military. They worked to get black people the same rights as white people, including equal chances to buy houses. In 1951, the NAACP launched its Equality (ee-KWAH-lih-tee) Under Law campaign. They believed that if schools were no longer segregated, then other places would become integrated as well.

Progress was very slow. Then, in 1954, the U.S. Supreme Court made an important decision. It ruled that segregation in public schools was illegal. Having separate schools for whites and African Americans **violated** (VY-uh-lay-ted) the U.S. Constitution. Schools had to be integrated.

African Americans hoped other things would change as well. Maybe they could integrate other public places—like buses.

ROSA PARKS
MONTGOMERY BUS BOYCOTT
At the bus stop on this site on December 1, 1955, Mrs. Rosa Parks refused to give up her seat to boarding whites. This brought about her arrest, conviction, and fine. The Boycott began December 5, the day of Parks' trial, as a protest by African-Americans for unequal treatment they received on the bus line. Refusing to ride the buses, they maintained the Boycott until the U.S. Supreme Court ordered integration of public transportation one year later. Dr. Martin Luther King, Jr. led the Boycott, the beginning of the modern Civil Rights Movement.
(Continued on other side)
ALABAMA HISTORICAL ASSOCIATION   1979

Rosa Parks worked with Dr. King (background) during the boycott.

A New Leader Emerges

Word about Rosa's arrest quickly spread among African Americans. Some of them asked Rosa to appear in court. They knew about the Supreme Court decision the year before. Maybe the court would agree to change the law in Montgomery. She was a respectable woman. She was married. She worked hard.

Other African Americans had been murdered for taking a stand. Rosa thought about the risks. Then she agreed. She was tired of being pushed around because of her skin color.

She was scheduled to appear in court on Monday, December 5, 1955. Montgomery's African Americans wanted to show their support for her. They decided to **boycott**

(BOY-kot) Montgomery buses that day. They would not ride the city buses, and the city would lose money.

It wasn't easy to take part in the boycott. Many people could not afford cars. They depended on buses to get to work. Some people had to walk miles to get to their jobs. Others rode with friends. But the people worked together, and the boycott was a success. Nearly every African American stayed off the Montgomery buses.

Rosa went to court. The judge listened for five minutes. He said she had broken the law and would have to pay a fine.

Rosa's lawyers were happy with the decision. Because she was found guilty, they were allowed to appeal the case. That means they could take the case to a higher court. They would argue that the law that Rosa had broken violated the U.S. Constitution. They hoped that this court would agree that the law was unjust.

That same evening, thousands of African Americans in Montgomery held a public

Dr. Martin Luther King Jr. outlines his plans for the boycott to a number of African American leaders in Montgomery. Rosa Parks sits in the front row.

meeting. A young **pastor** who had recently moved to Montgomery made a speech. He told the crowd it was time to stand up for their rights. When he sat down, the applause lasted for fifteen minutes. After his speech, the young pastor, Dr. Martin Luther King Jr., led the boycott. His leadership would make him the most famous civil rights leader in the United States.

A booking photo of Rosa Parks. She was arrested in December 1955 for refusing to give her seat on a Montgomery city bus to a white person. She didn't stop there. On February 22, 1965, she was arrested again for breaking an old law against boycotts. Many people were inspired by her bravery.

Rosa Wins Her Battle

Dr. King, Rosa, and all the other African Americans in Montgomery knew that continuing the boycott would be difficult. The people in charge of the buses didn't want to give in, even though the bus system was losing a lot of money. White shop owners were also losing money. Whites tried to make it difficult for African Americans to ride in cars that didn't belong to them. Drivers were arrested because police said they were picking up hitchhikers, which was against the law. Those waiting for rides were arrested for **loitering** (LOY-tuh-ring), or standing around. Many whites threatened to hurt African Americans. Some threw bombs. Business owners fired African Americans who boycotted buses. Because of an old state law

Many African Americans in Montgomery walked to work, regardless of the weather, in their support of the boycott of the city's buses.

against boycotts, some of the leaders were thrown in jail. Rosa and Dr. King were both arrested for boycotting the buses.

Nothing stopped the boycott. It went on, week after week, month after month. Finally the U.S. Supreme Court ruled that segregation on buses was illegal. The court ordered the Montgomery bus system to become integrated. The boycott ended on December 21, 1956. It had lasted for 381 days.

A Montgomery police officer fingerprints Rosa Parks in February 1956. She and about 90 other African Americans were charged with breaking an Alabama state law forbidding boycotts.

It was a great victory for the people of Montgomery. It was also a great victory for African Americans all over the country.

Dr. Martin Luther King Jr. had become famous. He went on to lead other drives for

19

Civil rights leader E.D. Nixon walks Rosa Parks to the Montgomery courthouse on March 19, 1956. She and the other leaders would be tried for holding a boycott. Dr. Martin Luther King Jr. was the only one who had to pay a fine. Nixon was one of many African Americans whose homes were bombed by angry whites during the bus boycott.

Rosa Parks rides in a Montgomery city bus on December 21, 1956, the first day that the buses were legally integrated. Nicholas Chriss, a newspaper reporter covering the event, sits behind her.

increasing civil rights for African Americans. Many white people became involved in the civil rights movement. It was dangerous work. Some workers, both white and African American, were murdered. Many others were hurt.

In the end, their efforts paid off. Many important civil rights laws were passed during the next few years.

Rosa Parks as she appeared in 1964, the year President Lyndon B. Johnson signed the Civil Rights Act. This new law made it illegal to segregate schools and other public places in the United States. It also made discrimination illegal.

Rosa's Later Life

Rosa and Ray Parks left Montgomery in 1957. Both of them had been fired from their jobs soon after Rosa's arrest. They received many threatening telephone calls.

They moved to Detroit, Michigan. Ray got another job as a barber. Rosa did volunteer work for the NAACP. She often spoke to large groups about the civil rights movement.

In 1965 she was hired by John Conyers, a representative to the U.S. Congress. Rosa worked in his office in Detroit. Meanwhile, she continued to make speeches.

Ray died in 1977. To honor him, Rosa founded the Raymond and Rosa Parks Institute for Self-Development in 1987. The organization helps young people reach their goals, become leaders, and find ways to help others.

In 1988, Rosa **retired** from her regular job, but she continued to make public appearances. She was very famous. Many people called her the Mother of the Civil Rights Movement.

Not everything went well for her. In 1994, she was robbed. The thief took $53 in cash and beat her. It took a long time for her to recover. She almost lost her apartment in 2002 when she couldn't pay the rent. Then the company that owned the building allowed her to live there rent-free.

By then Rosa had received many honors. President Bill Clinton awarded her the Presidential (preh-zih-DEN-chul) Medal of Freedom in 1996. Three years later, Congress voted to give her the Congressional (kun-GREH-shuh-nul) Gold Medal. In 2000, *Time* magazine listed her as one of the 100 most important people of the twentieth century.

President Bill Clinton shares the spotlight with Rosa Parks at a Congressional Black Caucus dinner in Washington, D.C., in 1996. Earlier, Clinton had presented her with the Medal of Freedom, the nation's highest civilian (sih-VIL-yun) honor. The award recognized her lifetime of work for the cause of civil rights.

On June 15, 1999, Vice President Al Gore presented Rosa with the Congressional Gold Medal. Like the Medal of Freedom, it recognizes people who have done outstanding service to the United States. Gore said, "As we look at what she has done and what she is still doing, we need to honor her."

Mourners file past the casket of Rosa Parks as it lies in the Rotunda of the U.S. Capitol Building, October 31, 2005, in Washington, D.C.

Rosa Parks died on October 24, 2005. Her casket was taken to the Capitol Building in Washington, D.C. For two days, thousands of people streamed by to pay their respects. Only about thirty other people have received this high honor. Most have been presidents. Rosa was the first woman to be so honored.

Rosa Parks worked for civil rights for many years—both before and after her arrest on December 1, 1955. But she will continue to be remembered for her bravery on that particular day, for standing up by refusing to stand up.

CHRONOLOGY

1913 Rosa Louise McCauley is born on February 4 in Tuskegee, Alabama.

1915 She moves to her grandparents' farm in Pine Level, Alabama, with her mother and brother, Sylvester.

1924 She begins school at the Montgomery Industrial School for Girls, where she learns how to sew.

1929 She leaves school to take care of her sick grandmother.

1932 She marries Raymond Parks.

1934 She receives her high school diploma.

1943 She and Ray join the NAACP.

1955 She sparks the Montgomery bus boycott by refusing to surrender her seat to a white man.

1957 She and Ray move to Detroit, Michigan.

1965 Rosa begins working for U.S. Representative John Conyers.

1977 Raymond dies.

1987 Rosa founds the Raymond and Rosa Parks Institute for Self-Development.

1988 Rosa retires from working for Representative Conyers.

2005 Rosa dies on October 24. Memorial services are held for her in Washington, D.C.; Detroit, Michigan; and Montgomery, Alabama.

TIMELINE IN HISTORY

1619 First black slave in the original 13 colonies arrives in Virginia.

1857 In the Dred Scott decision, the U.S. Supreme Court rules that no slave can be a U.S. citizen.

1863 President Abraham Lincoln's Emancipation Proclamation frees the slaves in rebellious states.

1864 Sojourner Truth, a former slave and a speaker against slavery, works at a government refugee camp for freed slaves in Virginia; she meets President Abraham Lincoln.

1896	U.S. Supreme Court rules that segregation in public places is legal.
1900	Booker T. Washington founds the National Negro Business League in Tuskegee, Alabama.
1940	Tuskegee Institute begins training 1,000 black pilots, who will become America's first black military airmen.
1948	President Harry S Truman officially integrates the U.S. armed forces.
1954	U.S. Supreme Court rules that segregation in schools is illegal.
1963	Martin Luther King Jr. delivers his "I have a dream" speech.
1964	Three young white men are killed in Mississippi while working to teach blacks in the South about their rights. Congress passes the Civil Rights Act. Martin Luther King Jr. receives the Nobel Peace Prize.
1965	Civil rights leader Malcolm X is assassinated.
1968	Martin Luther King Jr. is assassinated.
1972	African American Senator Shirley Chisholm from New York runs for U.S. president.
1976	Black History Month is established.
1984	African American Jesse Jackson runs for U.S. president. He will run again in 1988.
1986	U.S. Congress establishes Martin Luther King Jr. Day, the third Monday in January.
1998	U.S. Congress passes the Hate Crimes Prevention Act of 1998.
2001	Colin Powell becomes the first African American in U.S. history to hold the office of secretary of state.
2005	Condoleezza Rice becomes the first African American female to become secretary of state.
2007	African American Barack Obama announces that he will run for U.S. president.

FIND OUT MORE

Books

Edwards, Pamela Duncan. *The Bus Ride That Changed History: The Story of Rosa Parks.* Boston: Houghton Mifflin, 2005.

Giovanni, Nikki. *Rosa.* New York: Henry Holt and Company, 2005.

Parks, Rosa, and Jim Haskins. *I Am Rosa Parks.* New York: Puffin, 1999.

Weidt, Maryann N. *Rosa Parks.* Minneapolis, Minnesota: Lerner Publications Company, 2003.

Works Consulted

Brinkley, Douglas. *Rosa Parks.* New York: Viking, 2000.

Dove, Rita. "TIME 100: Rosa Parks." *Time* Magazine. June 14, 1999. http://www.time.com/time/time100/heroes/profile/parks01.html

Fowler, Bree. "Rosa Parks, Civil Rights Pioneer, Dies at Home at Age 92 of Natural Causes." Associated Press. October 25, 2005.

Jahn, Gunnar. The Nobel Peace Prize 1964—Presentation Speech. http://nobelprize.org/nobel_prizes/peace/laureates/1964/press.html

Kohl, Herbert. *She Would Not Be Moved.* New York: The New Press, 2005.

Parks, Rosa. *Quiet Strength: The Faith, the Hope, and the Heart of a Woman Who Changed a Nation.* Grand Rapids, Michigan: Zondervan Publishing, 1994.

On the Internet

The Courage of Rosa Parks
http://www.nationalgeographic.com/ngkids/9802/rosaparks/

The My Hero Project—Rosa Parks
http://myhero.com/myhero/hero.asp?hero=rosaParks

My Story: Rosa Parks
   http://teacher.scholastic.com/rosa/
National Women's Hall of Fame: Women of the Hall
   http://www.greatwomen.org/
   women.php?action=viewone&id=117
Rosa Parks: The Woman Who Changed a Nation
   http://www.grandtimes.com/rosa.html

GLOSSARY

boycott (BOY-kot)—Organized refusal to do business with a person or organization.

diploma (dih-PLOH-muh)—Official paper showing that a person has graduated from a school.

discrimination (dis-krih-mih-NAY-shun)—Treating people differently because of religion, skin color, or other factors.

integrated (IN-tuh-gray-ted)—Including people of different races and groups, and treating them the same.

loitering (LOY-tuh-ring)—Hanging around in a public place for a long time without any reason for being there.

pastor (PAS-tur)—The leader of a church.

seamstress (SEEM-stress)—A person who sews.

segregation (seh-greh-GAY-shun)—Keeping people in different groups or races apart from each other.

violated (VY-uh-lay-ted)—Broke (a law); did not respect.

INDEX